Old Newburgh-on-Ytl

Janet Jones

Text © Janet Jones, 2015.
First published in the United Kingdom, 2015,
by Stenlake Publishing Ltd.
01290 551122
www.stenlake.co.uk

Printed by
Berforts, 17 Burgess Road, Hastings, TN35 4NR

ISBN 9781840337303

**The publishers regret that they cannot supply
copies of any pictures featured in this book.**

Acknowledgements

Thanks to Charles Catto, Margot Wright, Hazel Stuart, Ian and Rosie Nicol, Martyn Gorman, Ian Cruickshank, Gordon Raffan and Sandy Anderson for their help.

Bibliography

The Early Life of James McBey, An autobiography, 1883-1911, OUP 1977.
Aberdeen Journal, Aberdeen Evening Express, Aberdeen Peoples Journal, Aberdeen Weekly Journal accessed in The British Newspaper Archive.
The Statistical Account for Scotland 1791-99 edited by Sir John Sinclair.
New Statistical Account for Scotland 1834-45.
The Ythan: a river of history, Dave Raffaelli.
The Aberdeen Colliers, Peter Myers, 1987.
Newburgh's Sea-Faring Days, Peter Myers, 1977.
The Fortified House in Scotland, Nigel Tranter, 1965.
Newburgh Station 1877-1965, William Guild.
Newburgh Mathers School Log Book.
The Clyack Sheaf, David Toulmin, 1986.
Newburgh-on-Ythan Yesterday and Today, Jessie McPherson.
The Life and Death of Jamie Fleeman; the Laird of Udny's Fool, J. B. Pratt.
For You I Remember, Edith Bishop, 1980.

Introduction

These days, the village of Newburgh, some twelve miles north of Aberdeen, is a haven for bird watchers, anglers or walkers and there are few, if any, indications that for centuries it was a busy port with ships from Holland, Germany, Scandinavia, Wales and the north of England calling regularly with cargoes of lime, timber, slate, bones and coal and leaving again loaded with locally grown grain.

In the 16th century, much of Newburgh's success as a port derived from cheaper dues in comparison with those demanded by Aberdeen – a situation which Aberdeen Town Council found intolerable and in 1573 tried to remedy by confiscating the sails of any trading vessels in the harbour. For how long any ships were immobilised is not recorded.

During the 1700s, Newburgh seems to have been relatively prosperous. The village boasted seven fishing boats and supported some 200 inhabitants. By the end of the century however, the Rev. Mr. William Duff in the first *Statistical Account of Scotland* could only describe it as "a very dirty place" and "unaccountably neglected". Among the reasons for Newburgh's decline may have been poor fishing returns, smuggling, few employment prospects and the high price of fuel which forced many inhabitants to leave to find work in Aberdeen or go further afield to the New World. By the mid 1800s however, the population had risen from less than 200 in 1790 to 560. Agricultural fertilisers imported by sea had brought about improved crop yields in fields which earlier "were neither dressed, nor had they any interval of rest, but carried perpetual crops of grain to the utter impoverishment of the ground." This in turn brought more money into the area and by 1861 the *Statistical Report* could record a population of 570 and a village which supported "several merchants who deal in grocery and haberdashery goods and in ship stores, a baker, a butcher, shoemakers, tailors, blacksmiths and carpenters." There was also a bone mill owned by Messrs Black which ground the bones brought in by sea.

In 1884 the loading and unloading of ships became much more efficient after a much-needed pier was built at the Inches by The Aberdeen Lime Company Ltd. Up until then, this operation had to be undertaken at low tide with horses standing up to their bellies in freezing water while the carts were emptied or filled. Between the mid 1800s until the mid 1900s, the firms Mitchell & Rae, millers, suppliers of seed, animal feed agents, importers of coal and fertilisers, and The Aberdeen Lime Company Ltd. also an importer of fertilisers, were the main employers in Newburgh. It was a difficult time for the village when Mitchell & Rae in particular closed its doors for the last time. The firm was officially wound up in 1978 and nearly all their records destroyed.

For centuries the plentiful supply of mussels from the estuary provided an important source of income for the village. In his account of the Parish of Foveran from the late 1700s, the Rev. Mr. William Duff refers to "the innumerable beds of mussels; which are sent to Aberdeen, and sold at 1/8d, the peck, not only for the table, but for bait to the fishers." It was not only in Aberdeen that mussels from Newburgh were used to bait the hooks on fishing lines. The women from Collieston and Whinnyfold further up the coast would collect them and carry them back in creels along the coastal paths. There the mussels were put into rock pools to keep fresh until needed. By the 1930s, many of the fishermen and their families had moved to Peterhead or Aberdeen where the larger boats provided a better living. Although over the years, Newburgh had a few local boats which went to sea, it never became important as a fishing port. Difficulty crossing the mouth of the Ythan, the shifting sandbanks and sharp bends in the river made navigation problematical. Dredgers kept a channel open for ships trading at the quay but, even so, wrecks and groundings were frequent – and had been for centuries. These days only the small boats used by anglers are seen on the river. Seals languish on the sandbanks and eider ducks eat the mussels. Executive flats have been built on the quay and there are some new housing estates. Apart from those employed at Oceanlab, Aberdeen University's field research station, most people commute to Aberdeen to work. Newburgh may not be the thriving sea-port it once was; it remains however a very pleasant place to live – that is, unless the sea mist descends.

Knockhall Castle to the north of Newburgh in the early years of the 20th century. The stone walls, the trees and the dovecot have long since disappeared but the rest of castle still looks much as it has done since it was destroyed by fire in 1734. This three storey L-shaped tower house, built in 1565 by Henry, 3rd Lord Sinclair of Newburgh, a great supporter of the Reformation, stands on high ground overlooking the Ythan Estuary. It was sold to John Udny of that ilk in 1633 and, with the exception of a short period when it was captured by a Covenanter party under the Earl of Erroll and the Earl Marischal, has belonged to the Udny family ever since. When the building was destroyed by fire in 1734, the clan moved to Udny Castle, their other property in Aberdeenshire. The castle was never rebuilt and remains a ruin. The story goes that it was Jamie Fleeman, the Laird of Udny's fule or jester, who discovered the fire. He alerted the gardener who, in turn, warned the rest of the household. Jamie then rushed to the charter room, seized the iron charter chest and threw it from a window, a feat worthy of the strength of three men. It was only when the gardener observed Jamie laughing to himself that he realised the housekeeper was still in the castle. Over the years, she had treated Jamie badly and now he was taking his revenge. As the gardener was a great favourite of Jamie's, he managed to persuade him to go back into the burning building and save her – which he did with very bad grace. The charter chest in the Great Hall at Castle Fraser, which Anne of Udny took with her when she married Charles Fraser, is believed to be the same chest Jamie threw from the window.

This was the first, and much needed, bridge over the Ythan near Waterside to the north of Newburgh. Until it was opened in 1877, the only means of crossing was by ferry or at low tide by horse and cart. In winter this was not possible and a detour of 8 miles by Ellon was required. The following description of the construction of the bridge appeared in the *Aberdeen Journal* in July 1877. It "is composed almost entirely of iron, the nature of the foundations not permitting a stone erection, consists of six openings or spans, each 50 feet in width, with a clear roadway of 14 feet between the girders. The total length of the bridge is 300 feet. The piers, which consist of groups of cast iron pillars – four to each pier – rest upon timber piles driven into the bed of the river to a depth of 20 feet, these piles being furnished with a covering of concrete about six feet deep. Owing to the strong current, great difficulty was experienced in placing these piles. The superstructure of the bridge consists of two lattice girders, made continuous throughout, and upon these cross joints of iron, placed about 3 feet 6 inches apart, are fastened. Upon these joints is a covering of buckled plates, and the whole is finished with a concrete road-way about 6 inches deep." The bridge cost just under £4,000, £2,065 of which was raised by private subscription, £1,500 contributed by The Ministry of Transport and £300 from the District Road Trustees. Attractive though the bridge was, rust and discolouration of the superstructure were ongoing problems as were the holes in the concrete road surface. A weight limit was imposed for vehicles crossing, a restriction which Mr. Alexander Knox of Dee Street in Aberdeen ignored in August 1914. He was found guilty before Sheriff Laing of having driven a heavy motor car over the bridge without the consent of Ellon District Committee and was fined 15/-.

By the 1920s however, it was becoming clear that the Iron Bridge was no longer fit for purpose as a combination of the unanticipated increase in traffic and corrosion caused by the salt water had made it unsafe. In 1925, when work began on the second bridge, the engineer in charge considered it was too dangerous for the twelve children from Waterside, who attended school in Newburgh, to cross. It was decided they should go to Slains School instead. The New or Middle Bridge, which was made of concrete, was constructed in 1926 at a cost of £23,000, almost twice the original estimate of £13,000. Although the clear headway had been reduced from 17ft to 10ft, at high water, it was still possible for small boats to pass underneath. But this bridge too became unsafe when sea water penetrated the poor quality concrete used to cover the steel reinforcements. Repairs carried out in 1970 failed to arrest the deterioration and in 1987, a third and much more substantial bridge was built. Although the foundations of the second bridge had become unsafe, the superstructure proved to be extremely strong and it took several weeks to demolish. The third bridge over the Ythan at Waterside was opened on the 23rd of November 1987.

The quay at Newburgh in the early 20th century. From the middle of the 19th century, the large group of buildings on the right belonged to the firm of Mitchell & Rae. The three stone granaries in the distance on the left belonged to the Aberdeen Lime Company Ltd. whose headquarters were at Blaikie's Quay in Aberdeen. Mitchell & Rae was established in 1858 when John Rae from Ellon paid £4,000 for the Newburgh Commercial Company, importers of lime, coal, bones and exporters of grain, and went into partnership with Alexander Mitchell of Kincraig, Foveran. The firm became a limited company in 1912 and was officially wound up in 1978. The Lime Company Ltd was established in 1837 and traded until 1941 when it ammalgamated with the Northern Agricultural Company Ltd and became The Northern Agricultural and Lime Company Ltd. As simply The Lime Company Ltd, the business specialised in manures and animal feeding stuffs. In 1869 they proudly announced that they were suppliers of both Peruvian and Bolivian Guano, Phospho Guano, Crushed Bones, Bone Meal, Dissolved Bones and Superphosphates. In Newburgh Michell & Rae was the more successful business of the two and became the main employer for over a century. They were seedsmen, meal millers, grain and coal merchants and suppliers of fertilisers. Newburgh was a busy port with ships, such as those in the photograph, bringing in cargoes from Wales, England, Holland, Germany and Scandinavia in and taking grain and potatoes out.

Both Mitchell & Rae and the Aberdeen Lime Company Ltd. owned ships. In the early days of trading, this elegant part iron topsail schooner named *Ythan* belonged to Michell & Rae. She was built in Aberdeen by A. Hall in 1837 and bought by Alexander Mitchell for £975. When she was sold in 1850, she was described as being able to "carry large cargo in light draught" so would have been ideally suited for the shallow waters of the estuary. An interesting feature of this photograph is the man-made sand jetty to the right of the vessel. This has long since disappeared but may well have been where, without blocking the quay, ships could wait in one of the deeper pools for a cargo – or perhaps for a tide high enough to be able to put to sea.

TUG BOAT ON THE YTHAN.

The photograph on the right is of Mitchell & Rae's steam tug *Despatch* which was used to tow lighters laden with coal, lime and bone meal from Newburgh to the Meadows near Ellon where the cargo would be stored in Mitchell & Rae's warehouses ready for distribution throughout the area. As she drew less than a metre, the *Despatch* was able to navigate the shallow upper reaches of the river. Skippered by William Park, the tug continued working until 1924 when it made more financial sense for Mitchell & Rae to use traction engines to transport goods inland.

The photograph above is of the *Despatch* towing their sailing ketch *Emma Louise* from the quay along the narrow channel in the river made navigable by dredgers such as the *Rockchime* of Leith. In the days before tugs, goods were brought up the river on flat-bottomed rafts using the incoming tide for propulsion. Men wielding poles eighteen to twenty feet in length, guided these rafts and pushed them back on course if they grounded. On the way, there were several staging posts where some of the cargo could be unloaded. When empty, the lighters were floated back to Newburgh on the outgoing tide.

On the left is of one of the many ships which came up the Ythan until the mid 1960s. The small rowing boats were used by anglers fishing for sea trout and salmon. On the right is Mitchell & Rae's coaster the *Anno* built for them in 1951 by Hall Russell & Co. Ltd in Aberdeen. The *Anno*, named by the company manager's daughter, served Mitchell & Rae for over ten years. She carried grain and potatoes to Hamburg, and brought coal back to Newburgh until she was sold in 1963. The company then chartered the ageing motor coaster *Ashdene* whose distinctive painted funnel markings of a red star on a silver band, made her easily recogniseable. The *Ashdene* was the last vessel to visit the quay in 1968.

Among the the Lime Company's ships was the three masted iron schooner, the *Alexander Nicol*, which traded from Newburgh for over 34 years. Their small steamer *Portlethen* was a frequent caller at the port, that is until she was wrecked after being driven against the pier in Peterhead Harbour in February 1923. Mitchell & Rae's first coastal steamers, the *Gem* and the *Ruby*, were built for them in the 1880s by John Fullerton & Co. Paisley. They were small and maneouverable so were well suited for the challenging conditions presented by the river. Just before the war, in 1913, the John Duthie Shipbuilding Company in Aberdeen built the coaster *Tillycorthie* for Mitchell & Rae. In March 1917, she was sunk by submarine gunfire off the Northumberland coast. Only a few weeks later, the *Gem* was mined close to the Orkneys with the loss of six lives. The Lime Company too lost ships to enemy action.

The iron foundry and smithy near the quay in the early 20th century. The business was owned by Mr. Maxwell Gordon Rae. At a bankruptcy hearing reported in the *Aberdeen Journal* in July 1902, Mr. Rae told the Sheriff Court that in 44 years of trading, the foundry had sometimes been a paying concern and sometimes not. He explained that 1877 had been a particularly difficult year as the premises were destroyed by fire. Prompt action by "earnest workmen" with buckets, however, had prevented the fire spreading to Mitchell & Rae's Granary and Mr. Thomas Pyper's Wool Yard which were close by. The hearing concluded that Mr. Rae had sufficient assets to continue trading.

THE YTHAN ESTUARY, NEWBURGH.

B.2026.

The Ythan Estuary and the dunes – an idyllic place to walk, watch eider ducks and seals. But the river is not always as benign as it looks here. When Newburgh was a busy port, incoming ships had to cross the notorious Ythan Bar (mouth) which is the white line in the middle distance. They then had to negotiate their way up a narrow channel in the river kept open by dredgers such as the *Rockchime*. This was only possible if their draught was 3 metres or less. Over the years, and particularly during storms or when there was fog, numerous ships came to grief at the entrance to the Ythan; the Aberdeen-built wooden schooner the *Billow* in 1863, the South Shields trawler *Ocean Prince* in 1896 and the Grimsby trawler *Siluria* in 1924 are only a few. When the *Billow* was grounded after a collision with another ship, she caught fire and her cargo of lime scattered over the river banks. Since then the area has been known as The Billows Lime. More recently on Christmas Eve 1987, the 1700-ton Bahamas-registered tanker *Christian* found herself stranded on a sandbank in the estuary. She was freed after several attempts by the tug *Lady Debbie* of Hull and, undamaged, headed for Sweden to pick up a cargo of oil.

The lifeboat *Alexander Charles and William Aird*, which came on station in 1887, was Newburgh's first R.N.L.I. purpose-built vessel. Until then any attempts to rescue ships in trouble had to be made with a modified local boat. The *Aberdeen Journal* reported that a crowd of over 500 people assembled on the banks of the Ythan to witness the naming ceremony and the launch. It cost around £70 per annum to maintain the branch. £40 came directly from the R.N.L.I and the remaining £30 was raised locally by subscription and fund-raising events. During the 19th century, the number of vessels using coastal waters increased rapidly due to the growth of the fishing industry and coastal trade and, as a result, groundings and shipwrecks became more frequent, particularly in the dangerous waters to the north and south of the Ythan Estuary. Aberdeen and Peterhead had lifeboats but their distance from Newburgh meant they were of little use in an emergency.

The *Alexander Charles and William Aird*'s first call-out when lives were saved was in 1892 when two seamen were rescued from the local vessel *Conqueror* as it broke up in heavy seas at the mouth of the Ythan. The second was in 1889 when the steam trawler *Gannet of Granton* became stranded on the north bank. Her crew of eight was brought back safely to Newburgh.

From 1877 until 1924 when the R.N.L.I. provided a tractor, the lifeboat and the heavy carriage on which it was mounted had to be manhandled from the boathouse to a suitable launching site on the river or, if that was not possible, to a point further along the shore. Even when horses were used, this was a fomidable undertaking. In his autobiography, James McBey wrote: "Easterly gales were frequent during the winter. If a rocket, fired from the lifeboat-house a mile distant, exploded above the village it was a signal that a ship was in distress and every able-bodied person had to drop tool or implement and hurry across the Links to man, or help launch, the lifeboat. The postman left his mail where he was delivering at the moment and the school was closed. To launch the lifeboat in the river was, as often as not, impossible, as the bar was a mass of curling breakers and the tide running in. The boat on its broad-wheeled carriage might have to be pulled for miles along the coast in soft sand and blowing spray which bit and stung exposed skin. Long ropes were attached to the carriage; everyone lent a hand and the procession pulled itself slowly towards where in the distance a tragic cluster of men clung to a broken mast on a hull slowly being pounded to pieces far out among the breakers." Every able-bodied person helped to launch the lifeboat. The women too played their part. After the difficult rescue of six seamen from the three-masted Norwegian schooner *Erik Giesson* in October 1915, the *Aberdeen Weekly Journal* reported "The Newburgh women deserve great credit in helping the men draw the lifeboat for nearly two miles along the sands to the scene of the wreck. They worked with a will and a few of them were several times up to the waist in water."

The *Ellen Newman and John Bentley* came to the station in 1889, a gift from Mr. John Bentley of London. She cost £300 and was larger than her predecessor, being a 31ft by 7ft 3ins wide self-righter, rowing 10 oars. In November 1889, the Danish brig the *Olga* of Roone, with a cargo of timber, became stranded on a sandbank south of the river Ythan. A heavy sea was running and, as the lifeboat approached, the ship began to break up. Two men clinging to wreckage were picked up and a further three from a small boat which sank soon afterwards. The lifeboat crew succeeded in manoeuvering through the cargo of timber and batons which had broken loose to rescue three more men and their captain. One man, unfortunately, was struck by a spar and killed.

The third lifeboat, the *James Stevens No. 19* arrived in Newburgh in 1901. She was one of a series of twenty lifeboats bought by the R.N.L.I. using a legacy received in 1824 from the estate of Mr. James Stevens, a property developer from London. With Coxswain John Innes in charge of this self-righting 34ft pulling and sailing lifeboat, the station began one of its most successful periods. Over 25 years, eight seamen were rescued from the steam trawler *Tillydene*, eight from the *Taymouth*, nine from the trawler *Bass Rock*, four from the trawler *Lord Ashley*, nine from the *Faith* of Aberdeen, six from the sailing vessel *Erik Giessen* and seven from the *Portlethen* of Aberdeen.

Perhaps the most outstanding rescue took place in October 1923 when the *Imperial Prince* of Aberdeen was driven ashore south of Balmedie. The *James Stevens No. 19* was dragged seven miles along the sands to a point opposite the sinking wreck. During the first rescue attempt, two men were saved while a third was washed overboard and drowned. Two more unsuccessful attempts were made before additional help was summoned and, with a crew comprising Coxswain Innes, his son James as Bowman and volunteers from two navel vessels from Aberdeen, five men who had been clinging to the rigging for over 13 hours were rescued. At a ceremony held in the Public Hall, Lord Caithness presented Coxswain John Innes with the R.N.L.I.'s Silver Medal for gallantry and Bowman James Innes with the Bronze Medal for gallantry. He also read out a letter from the R.N.L.I. recognising the contribution made by the women who had helped to drag the lifeboat along the beach.

Bowman James Innes

Coxswain John Innes

In 1926, the *John and Amy* came to Newburgh, a 34ft x 8ft pulling and sailing boat costing £600. She may only have answered three calls during her nine years in service but in that time was responsible for the rescue of the crew of ten from the trawler *Isle of Wight* when it became stranded in thick fog at the mouth of the Ythan. Although the lifeboat station had acquired a small tractor in 1924 to help launch the boat, it was not until 1932 that a purpose-built vehicle was made available. It was a modified Clayton fitted with a special Gerrard gearbox of R.N.L.I type which gave an enormous advantage when being driven in soft sand or mud. In addition, new types of hand-grips and footholds were incorporated in the body to ensure a greater level of safety for the launchers. The 40 h.p. Dorman engine was capable of pulling 30 tons in weight.

Coxswain Alexander Youngson took command of the lifeboat the *John and Robert C. Mercer* when it came to the Newburgh station in 1935. On the 28th of March 1941, the *SS Melrose Abbey*, a vessel of 1,900 tons with a crew of 49, became stranded after being driven off course. The lifeboat rescued 47 of the crew. The Master and the First Officer were saved by breeches buoy.

Costing £3,791, the *John Ryburn* arrived in Newburgh in 1941 and was the station's first motor powered boat. In addition to its crew of seven, it was capable of carrying sixteen people. Unfortunately, it was not a self-righter and when the vessel overturned in heavy seas while approaching the mouth of the Ythan on the 26th of January 1942, two of her crew were drowned. James Walker and Assistant Mechanic George White were dragged ashore by local people who had been watching the tragedy unfold but attempts to resuscitate them were unsuccessful. The remaining five crewmen, though weak from exhaustion, were unharmed. It was ironic that when the bodies of the dead men were being brought back to the village by tractor, a German bomber should attempt to bomb the bridge. Fortunately the attempt was unsuccessful. After the war, larger and more powerful lifeboats from Aberdeen and Peterhead were able to cover greater distances and the importance of the smaller lifeboat stations declined. The District Inspector of Lifeboats decided Newburgh should remain open on condition no more money would be forthcoming. Before the station closed in 1965 however, the *John Ryburn* participated in two further major rescues when twelve seamen were brought ashore from the *SS Holderness* of Hull and nineteen from the motor vessel *Ferm* of Gothenberg. Over the years, the Newburgh lifeboat crews rescued 153 lives, often in difficult and dangerous conditions.

A fancy dress party held in the 1930s in the Public Hall in the 1930s and organised by The Newburgh Ladies' Lifeboat Guild. The ladies of the Guild were active fundraisers for the Lifeboat. In February 1935, they put on two one-act plays, *The Salmon Poachers* by Joe Corrie and *No Hawkers* by Christine Orr and in 1936 they staged the Doric comedy *Tartan House* written by local author Miss E. I. Keith. On both occasions their efforts were met with an enthusiastic reception.

On the left is Culterty House in the mid 1800s with whale bones decorating the garden. Below is Culterty House in 1978 when it was a grace and favour house for the Regius Professor of Natural History at Aberdeen University. In the late 19th and early 20th centuries until his death in 1905, this was the home of Mr. James George Rae, one of the founder members of grain and coal merchants Mitchell & Rae whose premises were on the quay. Mr. Rae's son, Lieutenant J. Gordon Rae, was in command of the local regiment which acted as bodyguard to The Prince of Wales when he visited Udiapore in Central India in 1905. As were many of the larger houses in Newburgh, Culterty was sometimes let out to summer visitors. An advertisement from the *Whitstable Times* and *Herne Bay Herald* in May 1913 reads: "NEWBURH-ON-YTHAN, Aberdeenshire. For summer months. CULTERTY HOUSE, furnished 3 public rooms, 6 bedrooms, billiard room, bathroom etc. Garage, fishing, golfing, bracing sea air. Particulars, Mitchell & Rae." Later Culterty became the home of the eminent ophthalmologist and ornithologist Dr. Edgar Smith.

The artificial ponds in the grounds of Culterty House, which were fed from the river at high tide, attracted a wide variety of birds, particularly ducks and in September 1940, in order to raise money for the "Comforts Fund" for the troops, Dr. Smith invited the public to visit his Bird Sanctuary. Admission was 1/-.

Looking north towards the quay in the early 1900s. The large building in the background on the right is Mitchell & Rae's granary which was rebuilt and modernised at a cost of £13,000 after a devastating fire in December 1895. The masts protruding above the roof may well belong to the firm's coastal steamers, *Ruby* and the *Gem*. The chimneys are part of the bone mill where bones imported by sea were crushed to make fertiliser. Still on the right, the house facing the road is Prospect Villa, occupied at the time by Alexander Mitchell Rae who owned the blacksmith's shop at the quay. On the far left is Culterty House, home of John Rae, one of the mill owners. He operated his own generator making Culterty one the first houses in the village to have electricity.

The burial vault for the Udnys of Udny in the graveyard on the area known as the Inches. It is believed to date from around the mid to late 1700s and was built on the site of the old chapel of the Holy Rood also known as The Red Chapel. The names on many of the gravestones surrounding the vault reflect Newburgh's past connections with the sea. Shipmaster Robert Soang (died 1919) who skippered Mitchell & Rae's motor coaster *Gem*, river pilot James Crombie (died 1931), master mariner W.A. Logan (died 1942), shipmaster William Brodie (died 1800), shipmaster James Innes (died 1779), shipmaster William Burgess (died 1908) and shipmaster William Stephen (died 1916) are but a few.

The car from the 1930s is about to turn down the lane now known as Errol Place at the north end of Newburgh. The first building on the right was The Clydesdale Bank. Although there were banking facilities in the village as far back as the 1860s, it was not until the 1920s that this building, then named Errolbank, housed the bank itself. Until then banking transactions were carried out by agents such as Mr. Peter Murray who held the post for 46 years from 1873 until 1919 in his shop further down Main Street. Over the years, the bank had several incarnations. In the 1860s, it was The Commercial Bank. In the 1880s and into the 1900s, it was the North of Scotland Town and County Bank Ltd. In the 1930s, it was simply the North of Scotland Bank Ltd and finally it became a branch of the Clydesdale Bank. In the mid 1970s, the bank closed down and the building was sold. It is now in private ownership and called The Old Bank House. In the 1900s, Errol Place was known as Auld Inn Lane. There used to be an inn at the far end where Chevalier de St George, the Old Pretender, is thought to have spent the night of the 24th December 1715. He was on his way to meet the Earl Marischal from Fetteresso who, along with the Earl of Mar, hoped to regain the British crown. Nothing came of his plans however, and he left for France from Montrose in February 1716, a disillusioned man.

Main Street looking south in the early years of the 20th century. The building furthest away on the left is the Udny Arms Hotel. Set back from the road and just out of sight is Gleneden, home to several generations of the Logan family, many of whom had maritime connections. Next is Errol House, described by May Williamson in her essay on Newburgh as "a tall, grim-looking building". It was one of the many properties in the village which were let out to summer visitors and was demolished some years ago. Then comes Errolbank which later became the Clydesdale Bank. During the First World War, this was home to Commander Alec Henderson of the Royal Naval Reserve. After the war, he was appointed Marine Superintendent in Buenos Aires for The Donaldson South America Line. The curiously named Witch Hill follows, the residence in his retirement of Dr. Joseph F. Duncan, founder of the Scottish Farm Servants Union. Briarlea is next, the home of Private Gordon Stewart Smith who was awarded the Military Medal in 1918. Some years after this photograph was taken, Mrs. James Scorgie from Forvie Villa, the last house on the left, was killed by a car when she ran across the road after her dog. On the right of the picture is the gable end of Morrison's Buildings which, for a short time, housed the post office run by James Gibson.

Newburgh on Ythan, Aberdeenshire

Looking north towards the quay. On the left behind the trees is the imposing Newburgh House which dates from around 1800. It is unusual in that, unlike the other houses on Main Street, it faces south with the gable end to the road. Newburgh House was bought in 1911 by Thomas Fiddes Spalding, a native of Newburgh and retired shipmaster of the Aberdeen White Star Line. In 1866 Mr. Spalding joined the tea clipper *Queen of Nations* and began a four year apprenticeship sailing between London and Sydney. At the time, piracy was rife in the China Seas so all clippers carried guns. The *Queen of Nations* had six guns on her main deck with twelve muskets and twelve cutlasses being kept in case of sudden attack. During his 41 years at sea, Mr. Spalding made over 73 voyages to and from Australia and 27 voyages to Cape Horn. At one time, he sailed in the Aberdeen-built *Thermopylae*, the clipper which beat the *Cutty Sark* in a race from Shanghai to London in 1872. His name is still remembered in Newburgh as he donated enough money to build one of the bridges over the Foveran Burn which connect the village to the links. In 2015, the Spalding Bridge, as it was known, was declared unsafe and is no longer in use. A great loss to the village.

During the first decades of the 20th century, Alex Sangster's bakery was opposite Errol House on Main Street. In the early morning, if the shop was still closed, it was possible to go in at the side door to buy a hot rowie. Mr. Sangster's wife, seen on the right, and his son Sonny helped him. He employed two drivers to deliver bread, biscuits and cakes all made on the premises.

The Udny Arms Hotel in the late 1920s. In the *Aberdeen Journal* of June 1869, Mrs. Allan announced that she had "recently built a large and commodious House, fitting it up as a first-class HOTEL, and furnishing it in such a manner as to secure the comfort of Commercial Gentlemen and Visitors". Among the attractions she listed "excellent fishing" and that Newburgh was "considered a healthy and bracing place with good sea beach for bathing". The "excellent fishing" on the River Ythan was the main attraction for generations of guests at the hotel, among them Crown Prince Vajiravugh of Siam and his four brothers who stayed for a month in 1898. For many years after their visit, Mr. Ritchie, the then proprietor, was able to advertise that the Udny Arms was "under royal patronage". The actor James Robertson Justice was a frequent guest as was James Scott Skinner "The Strathspey King". Wilhelmina Bell, the subject of Skinner's well-known tune *The Bonnie Lass o' Bonaccord*, was a waitress in the hotel. Edith Bishop, author of *For You I Remember* recalls the occasion she became lost when on holiday as a child in Newburgh before the First World War and was found playing with the pigs in the hotel pig sty. When the telephone exchange in Newburgh opened in 1922, it was Mr. Ritchie from the Udny Arms who made the first call. The now ubiquitous sticky toffee pudding made its first appearance on the dinner menu during the 1960s when the hotel was owned by Dr. and Mrs. Bates. The recipe remained a closely guarded secret for many years and diners would come from near and far just to sample its delights.

SEA TROUT CAUGHT BY ALEX. A. CRUICKSHANK 11TH JULY 1929 ON THE YTHAN AT NEWBURGH. LENGTH 34" GIRTH 18" WEIGHT 14¾ LBS.

Mr. Alex Cruickshank from Newburgh was so proud of the 14 ½ lb sea trout he caught in the Ythan in 1929, he chose to have it stuffed and mounted in a glass case rather than share it with friends and family round the dinner table. It is highly probable that at the end of his day's fishing he followed local tradition and took it to the Udny Arms hotel to weigh it on the large set of brass scales in the porch before recording his catch in the Fishing Book. Together with his name, he would have noted the kind of fly used, the date and weather conditions and, of course, the weight of the fish.

There have always been good years and not so good years for the quantity of fish in the river. In August 1915, *The Aberdeen Weekly Journal* reported that "the estuary is at present teeming with fish. Gentlemen fishing from the hotel are sending large quantities to the hospitals in Aberdeen for the wounded soldiers." 1929 too must have been a good year for large sea trout as *The Aberdeen Journal* reported that in May while "fishing the Udny Arms Hotel water, Mr. Thomas Walker hooked and landed a monster trout. This measured thirty-one inches in length and fifteen and a half in girth and weighed 10 ½ lbs. After a great struggle, Mr. Walker landed his trout, which proved to be in grand condition and fresh from the sea." At the time, his fish was thought to be a record for the Ythan – that is until Mr. Cruickshank caught his "monster" in July the same year. In 1950, *The Sunday Post* reported an angler had found sixpence inside a trout he caught on the Ythan.

The building with chimneys on the left is the corf house where salmon were cured and nets stored over the winter. The small building in the foreground and the mound beside it is the ice house where the salmon were stored. In a very cold winter, ice was taken from an area known as The Hauchie (low-lying water) beside the Fisher Briggie but more usually it was brought in by redundant whaling ships from Peterhead. The nets were hung on ropes attached to poles so that they could be mended and dried out. The salmon were caught in bag nets positioned at intervals both to the north and south of the mouth of the river. When the above photograph was taken, John Innes, skipper of the lifeboat and salmon fisher was in charge. During the salmon season, he often stayed in the bothie at Rockend. The Ordnance Survey map from 1902 shows there was a curling pond on the links near the corf house and a gravel pit.

This austere granite building on Main Street originally belonged to the United Free Church at Newtyle south of Newburgh. It was built in the late 1880s and was known then as The Free Church Mission Hall. When The Church of Scotland and the Free Church congregations amalgamated in 1929 and the Free Church closed for worship, the Hall became the property of the Established Church. These days it is known simply as The Church Hall and looks much as it did in the early 1900s when this photograph was taken in the early years of the 20th century. The red granite fountain, which was presented to the village by Mrs. Udny of Udny in commemoration of Queen Victoria's Diamond Jubilee in 1897, has been moved to a recess in the corner of the wall. It bears the date, the Udny family motto and arms and the inscription: "No gift on earth pure water can excel. Nature's the brewer and she brewed it well." During the Second World War, the iron railings in front of the hall were removed supposedly for re-cycling into munitions. It is now known that this was largely a propaganda exercise to give people a sense of having contributed to the war effort. The railings were replaced in the 1990s. In January 1934 the *Aberdeen Journal* reported that a fire had broken out in the hall at the point where the stove pipe pierced the roof. A chain of helpers on ladders passed up buckets to the fire fighters on the roof and managed to prevent any extensive damage.

The Public Hall on Main Street designed by architect Wm. Ruxton of Aberdeen. From the outside, with the exception of the water pump and the railings, the hall looks much as it did when it opened in 1891. The occasion was marked by a concert with artists coming from Aberdeen and Mr. Lumsden from Belhelvie giving an entertaining speech. £250 of the £640 required to erect the hall was raised when the people of Newburgh held a bazaar in 1890, the remainder coming from various generous benefactors, among them Mr. Andrew Carnegie who contributed £116 towards books for the library. The feu superior of the village, Mr. J. H. Udny, also made a donation and put the site at the disposal of the promoters at a nominal feu duty. According to the *Aberdeen Journal*, the hall was built to seat 500, 400 people downstairs and 100 in the gallery. There was also a small suite of apartments, one of which was a ladies' retiring room, the other a library. Four large chandeliers hung from the ceiling. In 1903, the hall closed for redecoration. The earlier terracotta walls were painted "a pleasing sea-green colour" and the ceiling covered in "stars with glittering golden centres". In 1933, the hall was refurbished again and electric light installed. To celebrate the occasion, people from the village held a dance with music played by The New Orleans Band. The gallery, the chandeliers and the library may no longer feature but the hall still provides a venue in the centre of Newburgh for clubs and concerts.

An almost traffic-free Main Street in the 1910s and evidence on the road that horses were still being used. The Mail Bus is heading into Aberdeen. It picked up passengers on the Quay Road in Newburgh and took them the 14 ¾ miles via Belhelvie and Balmedie Post Offices and Bridge of Don to the Schoolhill Station in Aberdeen. On the right is the chemist shop with the mortar and pestle sign above the door belonging to Fred McPherson. His son Bob and daughter Jessie worked with him while daughter Daisy helped her mother in the house. During the First World War, Mr. McPherson often treated people with minor injuries to save the doctor coming from Ellon. In February 1917, the Rev. T. McWilliam presented Mr. McPherson with a clock and a cheque for £31 "in grateful recognition of his ungrudging and helpful services in times of sickness."

Main Street before 1906 looking north. On the left, is the end wall of Holyrood Chapel. Next to Holyrood Chapel was the shoemaker, Soutar Benzie, or "Bangie Benzie" as he was known. Edith Bishop recalls that "he held court in the back shop, where he did repairs. There were usually a few worthies there having a discussion." It seems there were two tailors in Newburgh at the time this photograph was taken. There was Robert Taylor in Bridge Terrace who was also a professional golfer, and Henry Ironside whose shop was where the two women in long skirts are standing. Mr. Ironside's son Robert was lost at sea in 1941. His daughter, Mrs. Peters, ran the shop as a haberdashery until the 1980s, an Aladdin's cave of drawers containing threads and wool, warm vests and long-johns for the anglers on the river, buttons and cards of elastic. The smart appearance of the three boys suggests the photograph may have been taken on a Sunday when "Sunday Best" was worn. The design of the pram being pushed by the girl in black is typical of the early 1900s.

Over the years, the Post Office has moved up and down both sides of Main Street. In March 1906, Mr. Alexander Robert Imlach, watchmaker and supplier of fishing tackle, whose premises are shown here, was appointed sub-postmaster after the resignation of Miss Murray. "Watchie Pym" as he was known, was described by Helen Murray as "a very strict postmaster". On Pension Day, he would retreat to the back of the shop with a customer's pension book and place any monies due between the pages before returning with the book. Mr. Imlach kept a white cockatoo in a shed in the back garden and local children would chant "Come and dance. Come and dance" to make the bird move. He was also an accomplished photographer who turned many of his photographs of Newburgh into postcards. In the days before the telephone, keeping in touch with friends and family was done by letter so postmen such as Newburgh's William Hutchison, or Little Hutch as he was known, played a very important role in the community. A paragraph from January 1881 in the *Aberdeen Journal* shows how highly he was regarded. "The people along the road from Udny Station to and in Newburgh, wishing to show their appreciation of the obliging manner at all times, but especially the indefatigable exertions of the post-runner, William Hutchison, during this severe snow storm, he having never missed a day in delivering the mails, the distance for the double journey being fourteen miles, subscribed and presented him with a purse containing nine guineas."

The horse bus which ran from Aberdeen to Newburgh and back again until 1907, a trip which lasted three hours. The photograph was taken on King Street in Aberdeen. Sandy Blackhall, the driver seen above, held the position for over 50 years and, whatever the weather, wore a heavy army type coat and a lugged bonnet. It is said he always ate breakfast on the previous evening so that he would be on time in the morning. He liked to chew dulse, a variety of seaweed, a task made quite difficult as he had only one tooth at the front. Sandy was not only a driver, he also had a coach business in partnership with George Thomson of Aberdeen. In 1874, they announced in the *Aberdeen Journal* that they had agreed to amalgamate their coaches and "that no effort will be spared on their part to secure the comfort of Passengers and careful conveyance of parcels and Luggage." The Coach Office was at 6 Mealmarket Street in Aberdeen from where the bus started. It is clear from the photograph that the horses were overworked and underfed.

MAIL OMNIBUS, NEWBURGH. ABERDEENSHIRE.

The bus, registration SA 311, was owned by the Great North of Scotland Railway (G.N.S.R.) and ran between Aberdeen and Newburgh twice daily. "The Red Bus", as it was known, was capable of carrying ten passengers on the upper deck and ten on the lower deck and there were two open air seats next to the driver. In April 1907, the G.N.S.R. bought out Mr. Robert Deuchars of Strichen who had run the horse bus to and from Newburgh to Aberdeen since 1899 and instituted their own motor bus service. The company began to run into trouble during the war however when a combination of the rising cost of upkeep and high licence and taxation duties forced them to increase fares to a level an already cash-strapped public began to find unacceptable. Except in the summer months, the twice daily service became a once-a-day service carrying fewer and fewer passengers. In 1921, two enterprising ex-servicemen, Alex Cruickshank and George Ross, spotted the prospect of making a living by running a bus in opposition to the G.N.S.R. service and as a result "The Little Green Bus" became a familiar sight on the road. It was smaller, cheaper and more convenient. While the "Red Bus" charged 4/- for a return journey, "The Little Green Bus" charged 2/-. In 1922, the G.N.S.R. announced that it was suspending the Newburgh–Aberdeen service just as the owners of the "Little Green Bus" decided to put a second bus on the road to meet the increasing demand.

Cruickshanks Garage on Main Street in the 1950s. Until the last years of the 19th century, this was the horse bus station owned and run by the McBey family. They sold the business to George Cruickshank. In 1906, with so many horses to feed, Mr. Cruickshank bought the large farm Ythan Lodge just outside Newburgh but sold it again in May 1919 to concentrate on motorised transport. After he died in 1931, the business was divided into two. Alexander Cruickshank and his cousin George Ross ran the bus side and Alexander's brother John Cruickshank ran the livestock haulage side.

This imposing building has had two different lives, one as the village school and another as a chapel. The original school was established in 1838 by the trustees of locally-born John Mathers, a graduate of Aberdeen University, who emigrated to India. There he prospered as a surveyor and, by Deed of Testament, left £4000 from the interest of which £55 per year was for the clothing and education of twenty children of poor fishermen. As many of Newburgh's sons would earn their living as mariners, the trustees had a rigging mast with ropes erected in the grounds. But by 1881, the old school had become too small. In 1882 The Kirk Session bought the building and had a new school built further up Toll Brae or School Road as it became. The old school became Holyrood Chapel, not Holyrood Church, in commemoration of a much older chapel in Newburgh, the Red Chapel of Buchan, which belonged to the Abbey of Deer. The conversion to a place of worship took many years. A spire was added and, in 1890, Mr. James Gordon Stewart, a tea-planter in India, presented the Kirk Session with the turret clock and a bell which was brought to Newburgh by sea from South Shields. In July 1892, the congregation held a bazaar on the links to raise money to pay off the £200 debt incurred by the building work. Between 1906 and 1908, when the photograph on the left was taken, the chapel was closed while repairs to the roof were carried out and windows more appropriate for an ecclesiastical building were put in. Shortly before the reopening, a pitch pine pulpit with a canopy described in the *Aberdeen Journal* as being "richly and artistically carved" was installed and in 1913, a new pipe organ to replace the old harmonium inaugurated, the joint gift of Dr. Carnegie of Skibo and Mr. Duncan of Tillycorthie. Newburgh-born entertainer Dove Paterson donated the Britannia safety air-gaslight system, a complicated construction, with the power coming from falling weights erected in the clock tower. When wound up, these weights were capable of lighting the whole chapel. The 40 lights consumed around a quarter of a gallon of petrol per hour.

Mathers Public School, Newburgh.

Newburgh Mathers School replaced the earlier school in what is now Holyrood Chapel. In the background of the picture is the thatched roof of the old toll house.

The photograph, taken in 1906, is of head teacher William Williams with some of the older pupils. In the log book from the 18th of May 1903, Mr. Williams wrote that due to an epidemic (possibly flu) not many pupils were present. He also quoted from a recent H.M.I.S. report: "The only water is from a well in the public street. The serious attention of the Managers is called to the necessity of providing an adequate supply both for the lavatories and drinking purposes." In January 1904, he reported that attendance was again poor due to colds and in June there was an outbreak of scarlet fever. Measles struck in 1907, whooping cough in 1908, German measles and whooping cough in 1909; in 1910, scarlet fever reappeared and in 1912 many of the pupils went down with mumps. In 1907, the Inspector of Schools reported that "The infant mistress is overweighted. Some re-arrangement should be made whereby a more equal distribution of work may be between the three assistant teachers." Between 1912 and 1913, building work caused Mr. Williams to complain that there was "some inconvenience occasioned by stones, bricks and mortar and presence of tradesmen on the premises." By 1913 however he was able to report that during the session, "the School buildings have been much improved. A new water supply, enlarged porches and modern offices have been provided and a separate building has been erected for instruction in woodwork and cookery." At the time, there were four classrooms, two cloakrooms, two playgrounds and two outside toilets. Mr. Williams retired in 1922. The Education Act of 1872 made it mandatory for children between the ages of 5 and 13 to attend school and The Compulsory Officer was a regular visitor. It was noted that on Tuesday the 13th of December 1912, sixteen boys in the Senior Division were absent. They were believed to be beating at a hunt.

This photograph was taken in 1938. In March of that year, Domine Lyall, who had been appointed head teacher in 1935, wrote in the school log: "The whole school and indeed the whole village is greatly affected by the death of Rhona Gilmour, Police Station, Newburgh. Her winning smile, her vivacity and her happy spirit are greatly missed." Mr. Lyall was a strict disciplinarian. On one occasion, a pupil by the name of Jim Henderson who later drowned at sea, cut his finger on a chisel. Mr. Lyall belted him on the other hand and told him "That'll teach you to keep your hand behind the cutting edge." Jim returned to class still bleeding. He lived in what was known as the Poors House where families who had fallen on hard times found shelter. On the 22nd of April 1938, Mr. Lyall wrote "School roll 116. There are twenty five children absent with measles, ten contacts and five cases of mumps. There are only sixty four children present today." During the war, all children were required to carry gas masks or respirators as they were called. In June 1940, Constable Gilmour came to the school to make sure each child had one that fitted properly and Mr. McNaught, Assistant Director of Education, paid a visit to arrange for net curtains to be fixed to the window panes to prevent splinters of glass falling into the classroom should a bomb fall. During 1940 and 1941, studies were frequently interrupted by air raid warnings. When the siren sounded, the children were dismissed to find shelter in the village. On February 24th 1941, Mr. Lyall wrote: "There was an air raid warning at 10am today. We have now, with approval of The Director of Education, adopted a spotter system and carry on work when there are no aircraft in the vicinity." The entry in the log book on the 24th of May 1944 reads: "William Innes and Ed Aitken were given temporary exemption to plant potatoes at the farm of Knockhall. They did not return to school when the potato planting was done but remained to do other work. I went to the field and sent the boys back to school. I have warned the farmer that such action on his part must not be repeated."

NEWBURGH SCHOOL CONCERT.   CALLER HERRIN.

The photograph is of one of the concerts put on by pupils from Newburgh Mathers School in the early years of the 20th century. It shows the position of the original stage at the east end of the Public Hall.

POLICE STATION, NEWBURGH, ABERDEEN.

In January 1897, *The Aberdeen People's Journal* reported that "tenders amounting to £827 14s in all for the erection of a new police station at Newburgh have been accepted by the County Standing Joint Committee". The picture is of the new Police Station which was built on School Road in the early 1900s to replace the station on Main Street. In August 1916, the Newburgh constable apprehended three young fishermen from Peterhead in the act of taking 43lbs of coal from the quay. In court they explained that, as the weather was bad, they had taken the coal to light a fire on the links where they were going to spend the night. They intended to pay for the coal in the morning. They were each given the choice of paying a fine of £1 or go to prison for ten days. In September 1931, Aberdeen County Council approved the installation of a telephone in the Police Station and when electricity came to Newburgh in 1948, it was the first building to be connected. Newburgh no longer has its own policeman and the house is privately owned. The bars on the cell window are still there however, a memory of past times. In May 1858, the *Aberdeen Journal* reported that the cost of the police force for the County of Aberdeen for the past year was £2026 13/- 0d or an average of £49 8/- 7 ½ d for each constable.

According to Jessie McPherson, daughter of the chemist in Newburgh in the mid 1900s, there used to be 45 thatched cottages at the south end of the village. They were occupied by fisher folk who, Jessie writes, were "very religious and very kindly people, mostly Brethren". The women baited the lines with mussels and the men went to sea to catch cod, plaice, whiting and haddock. The women then dried or smoked the fish, packed it into baskets, which they carried on their backs, and set off on foot round the countryside to sell or exchange their wares at farms for butter, eggs and cheese, their baskets often as heavy on their return as when they left. In spite of the hard way of life, Jessie observed that "Many of this hardy race reached ninety and a hundred years." Although this photograph was taken on Main Street, most of the cottages were on or near Timmerlum Street, the name meaning Wooden Chimney Street. The chimneys in the photograph are clearly made of clay but at some point in the past, inside the house, a wooden canopy would have been suspended over a wide open stone hearth to guide the smoke towards an outlet in the roof. This outlet, which projected above the roof, was made of wood lined with clay and tied down with straw ropes. Local legend tells how during a severe snow storm, a certain Captain William Park was forced to climb out of his lum carrying a spade. If the story has any credence, this feat would only have been possible in the days before narrow clay chimney pots.

The south end of Newburgh in the early 1900s showing two of the larger houses on Main Street which are still there and one of the now demolished thatched cottages and gable end of the one next to it. Larger houses have replaced them. According to *The New Statistical Account* (1845) "The fine little burn of Foveran runs through the parish, and falls into the Ythan near the village of Newburgh. There are three meal-mills upon it, all of the best construction, and abundantly employed." The mills may not function any more but the burn still runs with a series of bridges over it connecting the village to the links and beyond. The girl in the photograph is crossing The Fisher Briggie. It is possible that the name arose because the Fisher Folk, who lived in the thatched cottages nearby, crossed it to reach the area of land where they hung fish on wires strung on poles or on racks to dry in the wind. In the 1900s, the burn became badly polluted with sewage and the Village Council agreed to having it cleaned out on a regular basis. They also decided to abandon the proposed costly scheme to build a dam to prevent sewage going up the burn. Several of the early Fisher Bridges which were built of wood were not sufficiently substantial to withstand the weight of water when the river was in spate and were washed away. The present one is made of steel and. although not as attractive, has been in place for many years.

Right: The Ythan Hotel on the left as it looked in the early years of the 20th century. The poles were for the telegraph and not the telephone which came to the village in 1922. The bridge was replaced with a wider structure during road realignment and the house in the centre, together with the small cottages in the background, have long since been demolished. The large house, known as The Bungalow, is still there.

Over the years, both the name and the appearance of the hotel have changed several times. According to the Ordnance Survey map of 1855-1882, it was known as The Ship Inn. By the early 1900s, it was The Ythan Hotel and in 2014 became The Newburgh Inn. To local people however, it has always been known as Briggies because it is in an area of the village known as Bridgefoot.

No record remains of when the hotel was built but it is likely to have been one of the "six or seven alehouses frequented by sailors, smugglers and fishermen" mentioned in the 1793 *Statistical Account* as it stands at the entrance to the village from the south and would have been the first port of call for thirsty travellers.

Close by, there used to be a house with a little gothic window nicknamed "The Caravan" because it had a flat roof. There was also a baker's shop.

Left: The Ythan Hotel as it was in the early 1950s. Mr. William Rennie, owner at the time, was one of three people in the village who installed a television in order to watch the Coronation in 1953. As the signal came from Kirk O' Shotts in the Central Belt, the picture was very grainy.

On the right is the Gallow Hill, the highest point in Newburgh. The white house is the Ythan Hotel and in the foreground the dairy farm Mill of Newburgh which belonged to Charles Catto until the 1960s. The large house on the left hidden by trees is The Bungalow on Main Street. The photograph was taken in the 1950s. In the past, criminals were hanged or burned on the Gallow Hill. It was there in 1597, Helene Fraser from Aikenshill was put to death as a "rank witch", a victim of James VI's belief that witches such as Helene were intent on murdering him. She was found guilty on "fourteen poyntis of witchcraft and sorcerie" by Foveran Presbytery. In the *Accounts of the Burgh of Aberdeen* there is a gruesome account of the costs of the different combustible materials used to carry out the sentence. On the south west slope of the Gallow Hill there used to be a gravel pit called The Meerie Hill. It has long since been worked out and is now the site of a modern housing development. In 1897, a bonfire was lit on the hill and on other high points in the Parish of Foveran to celebrate Queen Victoria's Diamond Jubilee.

A view of Newburgh from the Gallow Hill looking north in the early years of the 20th century. In the forefront are two small thatched cottages on Beach Road. One of them belonged to Jeannie Thain. Her father was a builder who was responsible for some of the houses near the quay. The large building on the left hand side of the photograph is The Bungalow. In the distance on the left is the school on the Toll Road (now School Road) which was built in the mid 1880s when the earlier premises became too small. To the right of the school is the Police Station and the large house facing south is Santa Cruz. Although not visible in this photograph, next to Santa Cruz was The Toll House, a small building with a thatched roof. Tolls were abolished in Aberdeenshire in 1865 and sometime during the 1910s, the Toll House was demolished to make way for a garden. The waste ground behind the six remaining fisher folk cottages on Main Street (and there are two more further up across the road) is where many similar cottages stood until they were taken down in the 1890s. The building with the spire is Holyrood Chapel.

Opening of Newburgh Pavilion, 1910.

By the early 20th century, Newburgh Village Council was aware that the village had become a favourite destination for holiday makers, particularly from Aberdeen and set about improving the amenities. One such measure was the pavilion on the links which was intended to provide shade when the sun shone and be a comfortable refuge on wet and windy days. It was the brainchild of Newburgh-born entertainer, Mr. Dove Paterson and both he and Mr. Ritchie from the Udny Arms Hotel were responsible for raising much of the £100 required for its construction. In the winter of 1909, Mr. Paterson held what the *Aberdeen Weekly Journal* described as "a grand entertainment" in Newburgh Public Hall while Mr. Ritchie "collected from every point of the compass and all ranks and conditions of men." At the opening ceremony shown in the photograph, The Rev. John T. Loutit, seen at the rear of the group, thanked Mr. Paterson and Mr. Ritchie for their sterling efforts to turn Newburgh into "The Brighton of the North" and, to considerable applause, suggested they might also consider providing the village with a cricket pitch and bowling green. Some five years after the opening ceremony, the *Aberdeen Weekly Journal* reported that children were "breaking the slates on the roof and digging the ground around it" and that "parents should endeavour to put a stop to the practice. If not, severe measures may have to be resorted to." Measures must have been taken as the pavilion stands to this day.

The photograph shows the original gates of The Foveran Parish War Memorial just outside Newburgh. The memorial was unveiled on Sunday the 15th of October 1922 by Principal Sir George Adam Smith of Aberdeen University. The names of the fifty five local men who gave their lives in the First World War were read out and inscribed at a later date on either side of the archway. One family named Gordon lost four sons. The Memorial is made of Hill of Fare granite and was designed by Mr. W. P. Duncan from Turriff. The new graveyard, seen through the arch, was dedicated on the same day on land acquired from the laird, Miss MacKenzie of Foveran.

Newburgh may not have been bombed during the First World War, but danger was never far away. In December 1918, *The Aberdeen Journal* reported, with just a hint of Schadenfreude, that "A German airship did once come within a dozen miles of Aberdeen; and to the north too. It had probably lost its way… It passed over the coast somewhere about Newburgh, was blown across the sea, and became a wreck on the shores of Norway."

They may not have been called to fight, but those left at home in Newburgh made their contribution to the war effort. In December 1915, *The Aberdeen Weekly Journal* reported: "Two little girls – Katie and Dolly Christie – Quay Cottages, whose father is a civilian prisoner of war in Germany – collected the sum of £1 19/- on behoof of Mrs. Niven's Christmas box appeal for prisoners of war in Germany."

In February 1916, the secretary of the parish of Foveran Red Cross Work Party forwarded the following items to the Central Depot in Aberdeen for distribution to those in need: "100 pairs socks, 5 pairs bed socks, 1 pair operation stockings, 2 pairs hose-tops, 13 pairs gloves, 1 pair cuffs, 1 pair draw-sheets, 20 mufflers, 1 dressing gown, 2 rubber hot water bags, 20 day shirts, 3 night shirts, 3 semmits, 2 pillows with slips, 4 suits pyjamas, 36 handkerchiefs, 18 pocket bags, 28 face cloths and 1 book." (*Aberdeen Weekly Journal*) The street lights were lit again in December 1918.

In July 1919, the *Aberdeen Weekly Journal* reported that "Peace celebrations in the Newburgh district of the parish of Foveran were held on the Links adjoining the village on Saturday afternoon. There were suitable games for old and young, and there were many competitors in each class. Dancing was engaged in on two large dancing boards granted by the Newburgh Highland Games Committee, music supplied by the Newburgh Band, and tea was served to all present."

Seventy years after the Second World War, reminders of the conflict are still visible in the dunes and on the beach at Newburgh. When German planes were spotted taking photographs of Aberdeenshire's coastline in 1938, it was assumed it was in preparation for possible invasion by sea, the flat sandy beaches being ideal for enemy landings. (Some accounts maintain the Graf Zeppelin photographed the coast in 1938 but as the airship was scrapped that year, this may, or may not, be accurate.) Chief Royal Engineer G. A. Mitchell, the man made responsible for coastal defences in the north east of Scotland, set about implementing a range of anti-invasion measures. Tank blocks made of concrete, such as those in the above photograph, were built along the beach and the estuary. Stones were set in the top to act as camouflage. Heavy gun emplacements (right) were built in the dunes. The gun-loops face inland as well as towards the sea should the enemy break through the first lines of defence. A number of pillboxes were positioned so that the men inside could see all the other pillboxes. And to this day, the remains of a kilometre-long anti-tank wall built of tubular steel scaffolding poles lie rusting in the dunes.

Foveran Church in the early years of the 20th century. This Category B-listed Georgian building, constructed in 1794 on the site of a much older medieval church, lies about a mile outside Newburgh. The manse, seen to the right, has been demolished and replaced by a more modern building. In his autobiography, the painter and etcher James McBey recalled that in the early 20th century "Religiously every Sunday forenoon all the villagers who could walk the intervening mile attended church service – a grim and solemn ritual. A strong smell of confined varnish pervaded the church and lent the service a characteristic flavour." The building contains some interesting artefacts, the most impressive being The Turin Stone on the west wall which commemorates two knights killed at the Battle of Harlaw in 1411. The knights are thought to have been brothers and grandsons of William de Turin who was granted the Charter of Foveran by King David II. Unfortunately, centuries of exposure to the elements when the stone lay outside in the churchyard caused it to crack. The delicate tracery outlining the depicted figures is still visible however. There are over 300 gravestones in the graveyard, the earliest dating from the mid-1800s. Many of the inscriptions such as those in memory of farmers and shipmasters, reflect Newburgh's links with the land and the sea. In 1936 the church underwent extensive refurbishment and redecoration. Pews and the communion table from the Free Church in Foveran, which had closed for worship that year, were installed. Sadly, regular services are no longer held in the church as parishioners now attend Holyrood Chapel in Newburgh.

62411   FOVERAN HOUSE, NEWBURGH.

This was built around 1771 by stocking merchant and sometime Provost of Aberdeen John Robertson of Pitmillan in the Parish of Foveran. It stands not far from the site of the Turing Tower, seat of the Turing Family and lairds of Foveran between 1359 and 1639. The Forbes of Tolquhon succeeded the Turings and it was during their possession in 1772 that the Tower fell down. Rather than rebuild, Sir Samuel Forbes decided to construct a mansion at Tillery on the west side of the parish on land he already owned. Following his death, John Roberston acquired Foveran Estate and set about building Foveran House and a second Turing Tower, seen here in the photograph, with stones from the ruin. The set-back wings either side of the house are much later additions as is the porch. After 1857, Foveran House and what was left of the estate went to members of the Mackenzie family. However, it was not until Miss Florence Mackenzie made it her permanent home after the 2nd World War that a member of the family stayed in the house for any length of time, preferring instead to remain at the London residence and let out the property in Scotland. In an article in *The Leopard* magazine in 1982, David Toulmin, wrote: "Miss MacKenzie became something of a bird in gilded cage: A Lady of Shalott in her ivory tower, isolated and almost feared by her indifference to strangers, so that very few people intruded upon her serene privacy. What it was like for an old lady living alone in that vast mansion is difficult to imagine, what with its ghostly cellars and subterranean stone passages, dark forbidding kitchens with their prison-bar windows; turreted stairways, labyrinthine corridors; the enormous rooms with their shuttered casements, pillared alcove and piano-key ceilings, marble fireplaces and walls in velvet textured paper – these were the style and pomp of a former aristocracy – latterly the reclusion of a lonely old spinster, companion of the cellar rats and bats of the Turing Tower." Florence Mary MacKenzie, the last resident laird of Foveran, died in 1973 at the age of 94.